Quick 'n' Easy

DESSERTS

A sweet treat, sugar fix or tempting morsel to satisfy a mood,

complete a meal or simply indulge in,

is the inspiration for this book.

How often do we need to rustle up something smart and

satisfying for a family meal or special occasion and

pore over our cookbooks then despair

because it's all too hard?

Simplifying methods for favourite recipes, taking new angles on

special flavours or simply being reminded of

some good basic places to start will be your inspiration

from the recipes that follow.

ISBN 1-877193-14-3

© Design & Illustrations –
Concept Publishing
© Text – Robyn Martin

Published in 1998 by
Concept Publishing
Fax 64-9-489 5335
Auckland, New Zealand

Written by
Robyn Martin

Photography by
Alan Gillard

Cover Photograph
Sweet Piroshkis, recipe page 45

Plates and bowls supplied by
Bloomsbury, Wellington

Layout & Type Imaging by
Hot House Design Group Limited

Recipes tested by:
Virginia McGregor
Linda Laycock
Kitchen Assistants:
Rosemary Hurdley
Kelli Craig

Printed in Hong Kong by
Bookprint International Limited

WEIGHTS AND MEASURES

All recipes in this book have been tested using New Zealand standard measuring cups and spoons. All cup and spoon measures are level and brown sugar measures are firmly packed.
Standard No 6 eggs are used.

TO SOFTEN PHILADELPHIA

The manufacturers of packet Philadelphia Cream Cheese recommend that it is softened before use.
To soften, allow to stand for 1 hour at room temperature, or remove from foil, place in a microwave in a microwave-safe bowl and microwave on high for 15 seconds per 125 grams.

* Trademark Kraft Foods Limited
ACN 004 125 071

Quick 'n' Easy

CONTENTS

The Shepparton Preserving Company (SPC) originated in Victoria, Australia in 1917 as a co-operative initiative by commercial fruit growers in the area. Since then, the SPC brand has maintained a strong commitment to supplying canned fruit of the highest quality. SPC fruit is picked when fresh but not over-ripe, and this, combined with their sophisticated canning process, ensure the best possible natural flavour and highest possible nutritional content for consumers.

SPC blends apricots, peaches and pears in natural juice, natural fruit nectar, lite juice and light syrup to suit all tastes and dietary requirements. There is also a 100% fruit range of apple, peach and apricot, wonderful for pies and shortcakes. The SPC range provides a variety of pantry essentials that are rich in vitamins with the added convenience of being inexpensive and available all year round.

When it comes to desserts, SPC fruit can be used as the main ingredient, topping or for presentation, offering consumers the variety and quality of fruit necessary to produce a wonderful array of desserts.

PHILADELPHIA CREAM CHEESE originated, as the name suggests, in Philadelphia, USA,
a city noted for the best quality foods. Philadelphia Cream Cheese was first made in
Australia by Kraft Foods in 1956 and has for decades been a household name, 'Philly cheese'.

Its rich, creamy texture and characteristic tang made it popular from the beginning,
and for many decades it has been the base of one of the world's
most enduring desserts – the cheesecake.

The versatility of Philadelphia Cream Cheese continues to grow. It is now widely used
for hor d'oeuvres, icings and main dishes as well as the favourite cheesecake,
and desserts such as the wonderful examples within these pages.

As well as the instantly recognisable and distinctive silver block,
Philadelphia Cream Cheese also comes in tub form in light and soft varieties.

LIGHT PHILADELPHIA CREAM CHEESE has the same great taste as the
classic Philadelphia with 30% less fat.

SOFT PHILADELPHIA CREAM CHEESE is a soft version of regular Philadelphia,
easy to spread straight from the fridge. A great substitute for other spreads,
Soft Philadelphia has half the kilojoules of butter and margarine.

Quick 'n' Easy

DESSERT CAKES

*A dessert cake is probably the most versatile of desserts.
It can be prepared well in advance, and even frozen
and freshened in the microwave or oven. It can travel well for
"take a plate" and can be served in a multitude of
sweet-eating situations.*

*Served with fresh or canned fruit and a flavoured cream or
yoghurt, even the simplest dessert cake can be transformed
into a deliciously memorable end to a meal.*

RHUBARB SLICE CAKE

125g soft butter

1 cup sugar

2 eggs

1 teaspoon vanilla essence

½ cup milk

1¼ cups flour

1 teaspoon mixed spice

½ teaspoon ground nutmeg

2 teaspoons baking powder

6 stalks rhubarb

TOPPING

¼ cup brown sugar

½ teaspoon mixed spice

¼ teaspoon ground nutmeg

70g packet slivered almonds

Place butter, sugar, eggs, vanilla, milk, flour, spice, nutmeg and baking powder in a mixer bowl. Beat on low speed to combine. Increase speed and mix on medium for 3 minutes. Pour into a baking-paper-lined 20 x 30cm deep cake tin. Cut leaves from rhubarb and discard. Trim ends and wash stalks. Cut stalks into 2cm pieces and place over the surface of the batter. Sprinkle over topping. Bake at 180°C for 50 minutes to 1 hour or until the cake springs back when lightly touched. Serve warm or cold, cut into slices.

TOPPING

Mix brown sugar, spice, nutmeg and almonds together.

Serves 6 to 8.

Rhubarb Slice Cake

MOCHA DESSERT CAKE

100g cooking chocolate

150g butter

1 cup sugar

1 cup strong black coffee

1 cup flour

¼ cup cornflour

1 egg

Cocoa

Mix chocolate, butter, sugar and coffee in a saucepan large enough to mix all the ingredients. Heat gently until butter and chocolate have melted and mixture is smooth. Remove from heat. Sift in flour and cornflour and add egg. Beat with a wooden spoon until smooth. Baking-paper-line the bottom of a 20cm round cake tin and pour mixture into tin. Bake at 160°C for 50 to 60 minutes or until cake is firm. Stand in tin for 10 minutes before turning onto a cooling rack. Serve dusted with cocoa and accompanied with fruit.

Serves 6 to 8.

CHOCOLATE MOUSSE CAKE

5 eggs

¾ cup sugar

100g cooking chocolate

100g butter

Chocolate curls

Separate eggs. Beat egg yolks and sugar until pale, thick and creamy and mixture holds its shape. Beat egg whites until stiff. Melt chocolate and butter and beat into egg yolk mixture. Fold this into egg whites. Baking-paper-line the bottom of a 20 x 30cm sponge roll tin and pour one-third of mixture into tin. Bake at 160°C for 35 minutes or until set. Cool. Pour remaining mixture on top of cooked cake and freeze until firm. Garnish with chocolate curls and serve with whipped cream.

Serves 6 to 8.

Mocha Dessert Cake (top),
Chocolate Mousse Cake

8

OTT DESSERT CAKE

This is a sugar fix cake that will make every sweet tooth fizz out. It is superbly decadent! We use bought sauces for this.

3 egg whites

¾ cup sugar

½ cup toasted ground hazelnuts

Whipped cream

Prepared caramel sauce

Prepared chocolate sauce

Fresh or SPC canned fruit

Beat egg whites until stiff. Beat in sugar until mixture is thick and glossy. Fold in hazelnuts. Mark two 20cm circles on a piece of baking paper. Spread mixture out to an 18cm circle. Bake at 150°C for 50 minutes to 1 hour or until meringue is dry and crisp. Cool in oven. To serve, fill and top with whipped cream. Drizzle over caramel and chocolate sauces and garnish with fresh seasonal fruit, drained canned fruit or a mixture of both.

Serves 6 to 8.

OTT Dessert Cake

SIENA CAKE

125g blanched almonds

125g hazelnuts

$^1/_2$ cup mixed peel

75g cooking chocolate

$^3/_4$ cup flour

2 tablespoons cocoa

1 teaspoon ground cinnamon

$^1/_4$ cup sugar

$^1/_2$ cup honey

$^1/_4$ cup water

Icing sugar

Roughly chop the almonds. Roast in a shallow baking tray at 160°C for 10 minutes or until lightly coloured. Roast hazelnuts at 160°C for 15 to 18 minutes or until skins begin to darken. Rub to loosen skins. Remove skins and chop nuts. Finely chop mixed peel. Roughly chop chocolate. Sift flour, cocoa and cinnamon into a bowl. Mix in nuts, chocolate and peel. Put sugar, honey and water in a saucepan. Stir over low heat until sugar dissolves. Increase heat and bring the mixture to the boil, stirring constantly. Boil without stirring until the soft ball stage. This is when a drop of mixture forms a soft ball in cold water. Mix the sugar mixture and chocolate into the flour and nut mixture until combined. Working quickly, spread into a baking-paper-lined 20cm sponge sandwich tin. Smooth the top with the back of a wet spoon. Bake at 160°C for 35 to 40 minutes. Cool in the tin. Dust with icing sugar and serve cut into thin wedges.

Serves 10 to 12.

Apricot Cake, Siena Cake and Lemon Semolina Cake

LEMON SEMOLINA CAKE

Semolina is usually found in the supermarket bulk bins or in packets in the cereal or baking needs section of the supermarket.

125g butter

1 cup sugar

3 eggs

2 teaspoons grated lemon rind

½ cup semolina

1 cup flour

2 teaspoons baking powder

¼ cup lemon juice

¼ cup icing sugar

Melt butter in a saucepan large enough to mix all the ingredients. Remove from heat and mix in sugar. Add eggs, lemon rind and semolina. Beat until well combined. Sift flour and baking powder into mixture and mix thoroughly. Pour into a baking-paper-lined 20cm round cake tin. Bake at 180°C for 35 minutes. Mix lemon juice and icing sugar together. Remove cake from oven and pour over lemon juice mixture. Return to oven and bake for a further 10 minutes. Serve warm or at room temperature with lemon flavoured yoghurt.

Serves 6 to 8.

APRICOT CAKE

2 x 415g cans SPC Apricot Halves in Natural Juice

125g butter

1 cup sugar

2 eggs

2 cups flour

4 teaspoons baking powder

TOPPING

¼ cup flour

¼ cup rolled oats

2 tablespoons brown sugar

1 teaspoon baking powder

50g butter

Purée one can of apricots and juice in a food processor or blender. Drain second tin of apricots. Melt butter in a saucepan large enough to mix all the ingredients. Stir in sugar and beat in eggs, flour, baking powder and apricot purée with a wooden spoon. Pour into a baking-paper-lined 20cm round deep cake tin. Arrange drained apricots over surface of cake. Sprinkle with topping. Bake at 180°C for 1 hour or until an inserted skewer comes out clean. Serve warm with whipped cream.

TOPPING

Mix flour, rolled oats, brown sugar and baking powder together. Rub in butter until mixture resembles coarse crumbs.

Serves 8 to 10.

FIG AND ROASTED ALMOND CAKE

Roast almonds at 180°C for 7 to 10 minutes. Roasted or toasted nuts have much better flavour and texture in any dish.

1 cup chopped figs

½ cup boiling water

1 cup roasted almonds

4 egg whites

½ cup brown sugar

1 tablespoon icing sugar

½ teaspoon cinnamon

SPICED CREAM

300ml cream

1 teaspoon cinnamon

Cook figs in boiling water for 10 minutes. Cool. Mix in almonds. Beat egg whites and brown sugar together until stiff peaks form. Fold figs and almonds into meringue. Spread into a 20cm round baking-paper-lined loose-bottom cake tin. Bake at 180°C for 45 minutes or until lightly golden and set. Cool for 10 minutes before removing from tin. When ready to serve, mix icing sugar and cinnamon together. Sprinkle over cake. Serve with spiced cream.

SPICED CREAM

Beat cream and cinnamon until soft peaks form.

Serves 6 to 8.

ITALIAN FIG CAKE

2 eggs

¾ cup sugar

1 cup flour

1½ teaspoons baking powder

¼ cup milk

1 tablespoon toasted breadcrumbs

Icing sugar

FILLING

1½ cups chopped dried figs

¾ cup finely chopped walnuts

¼ cup marmalade

2 teaspoons grated orange rind

⅛ teaspoon ground cloves

½ teaspoon ground cinnamon

Beat eggs and sugar together until light and thick. Sift flour and baking powder and fold alternately with milk into the cake batter. Grease sides and baking-paper-line the bottom of a 20cm cake tin. Sprinkle with the breadcrumbs. Spoon half the cake batter into the cake tin. Carefully dot fig filling over the top and spread over the cake batter. Pour remaining batter over the top. Bake at 180°C for 35 to 40 minutes or until an inserted skewer comes out clean. Dust with icing sugar. Serve warm as a dessert cake or cold with tea or coffee.

FILLING

Mix all ingredients together.

Serves 6.

ESPRESSO CAKE

1 cup boiling water

¼ cup ground espresso coffee beans

200g butter

1 ¼ cups sugar

3 eggs

1 tablespoon vanilla essence

2 cups flour

3 teaspoons baking powder

¼ cup finely ground espresso coffee beans

8 sugar cubes

Cinnamon

COFFEE FLAVOURED CREAM

300ml cream

1 tablespoon icing sugar

2 tablespoons very strong espresso coffee

Pour boiling water over first measure of ground coffee and leave to steep for 5 minutes. Strain liquid from beans and pour over butter in a large bowl, stirring until butter melts. Mix in sugar, eggs and vanilla and beat with a wooden spoon until combined. Sift flour and baking powder into mixture and mix in with second measure of coffee. Pour the mixture into a baking-paper-lined 20cm square cake tin. Bake at 180°C for 50 to 55 minutes or until cake springs back when lightly touched. Crush sugar cubes. Sprinkle over hot cake. Cool in tin for 10 minutes before turning onto a cooling rack. Dust with cinnamon and serve with coffee flavoured cream.

COFFEE FLAVOURED CREAM

Whip cream until soft. Beat in icing sugar and coffee.

Serves 8 to 10.

*Fig and Roasted Almond Cake,
Espresso Cake and
Italian Fig Cake (left)*

13

RUTH'S RUM AND RAISIN TORTE

1 cup raisins

2 tablespoons rum

1 cup chopped walnuts

3 egg whites

½ cup caster sugar

Icing sugar

Heat raisins and rum together until boiling. Remove from heat and set aside to cool while preparing remaining ingredients. Mix in walnuts. Beat egg whites until stiff. Gradually beat in sugar, beating until stiff, glossy meringue forms. Fold raisin mixture in. Spread into a 20cm round baking-paper-lined sponge tin. Bake at 160°C for 45 minutes or until firm to the touch. Cool in tin. When cold dust with icing sugar. Serve cut into wedges.

Serves 6.

HARLEQUIN BROWNIES

250g packet Kraft* Philadelphia
    Cream Cheese

½ cup sugar

2 eggs

1 teaspoon vanilla essence

200g butter

¼ cup cocoa

1 cup sugar

2 eggs

¾ cup flour

1 teaspoon baking powder

Soften cream cheese (see page 2) and mix with sugar, eggs and vanilla until smooth. Set aside. Melt butter in a large saucepan. Mix in cocoa. Remove from heat and add sugar and eggs. Beat until smooth. Sift in flour and baking powder. Mix until smooth. Pour half the chocolate mixture into a baking-paper-lined 20 x 30cm sponge roll tin. Arrange dollops of cream cheese mixture over the top of chocolate mixture. Pour over remaining chocolate mixture. Swirl a knife through the mixtures to marble the brownie. Bake at 180°C for 30 minutes or until brownie springs back when lightly touched. Serve with fruit and chocolate sauce.

Serves 8 to 10.

*Dessert Platter,
Orange Cream Spread,
Little Nut Bouches,
Ruth's Rum and Raisin Torte
and Harlequin Brownies*

DESSERT PLATTER

This is not a dessert cake as such but it fits the same sort of dessert need as a cake fills. I thought it a good idea and it didn't fit anywhere else in the book.

SWEET HEARTS

2 sheets sweet short pastry

Icing sugar

Fresh fruit

Cut small heart shapes from pastry. Bake on a baking-paper-lined oven tray at 190°C for 7 to 10 minutes or until lightly golden. Cool on a cooling rack and dust with icing sugar. Serve with orange cream spread and fresh fruit.

Makes about 46.

ORANGE CREAM SPREAD

If you don't have liqueur on hand, simply leave it out.

250g pot Kraft Soft Philadelphia Spreadable Cream Cheese

1 teaspoon grated orange rind

1 tablespoon orange juice concentrate

1 tablespoon orange liqueur

Shreds of orange rind

Mix into cream cheese the orange rind, orange juice and liqueur. Mix until smooth and pack into a small serving dish. Garnish with shreds of orange rind.

Makes 1 cup.

LITTLE NUT BOUCHES

2 sheets sweet short pastry

50g butter

³/₄ cup brown sugar

1 egg

1 teaspoon almond essence

¹/₂ cup chopped roasted almonds

Cut 5cm rounds from pastry and line mini patty or muffin pans with them. Melt butter in a medium saucepan. Remove from heat and mix in brown sugar, egg, almond essence and almonds. Three-quarters fill the pastry cases with nut mixture. Bake at 170°C for 15 to 20 minutes or until pastry is golden and filling set.

Makes 30.

15

Quick 'n' Easy
CHEESECAKES

Baked or chilled, cheesecakes have to be one of the simplest of
desserts and one of the most enjoyed.

With the help of a food processor to do your mixing, the time
needed to put a cheesecake together is minimal.
If you don't have one of these machines,
making sure your cream cheese is soft before you start
will make mixing by hand much easier.

Many of the cheesecakes featured can be used as basic recipes,
providing the opportunity to add flavours of your choice
as different ingredients become available and
seasons influence your food preferences.

APPLE CREAM CHEESECAKES

8 coconut biscuits

250g pot Kraft Soft Philadelphia
    Spreadable Cream Cheese

3 eggs

$^3/_4$ cup sugar

1 cup cream

415g can SPC 100% Apple

2 teaspoons grated lemon rind

2 tablespoons gelatin

$^1/_2$ cup sweet white wine

Apple slices

Toasted coconut

Place a biscuit in the base of eight baking-paper-lined half-cup capacity ramekins. Beat cream cheese with eggs and sugar until smooth. Whip cream until soft peaks form. Fold into cream cheese mixture with apple and lemon rind. Soften gelatin in wine. Stand over hot water until gelatin dissolves. Mix into cream cheese mixture. Divide mixture among ramekins. Refrigerate until set. Run a knife around the edge of the ramekin. Turn onto serving plates. Serve garnished with apple slices and toasted coconut.

Serves 8.

SUPER QUICK BISCOTTI CHEESECAKES

125g Kraft Soft Philadelphia
    Spreadable Cream Cheese

1 tablespoon orange flavoured liqueur

2 tablespoons strawberry jam

16 pieces almond biscotti

8 large strawberries

$^1/_4$ cup chocolate sauce

Mix cream cheese, liqueur and jam together. Spread thickly over biscotti. Top with strawberries and drizzle over chocolate sauce.

Serves 6 to 8.

*Super Quick Biscotti Cheesecakes
and Apple Cream Cheesecakes*

WALNUT AND DATE CHEESECAKE

250g packet malt biscuits

75g butter

FILLING

1 cup chopped dates

¼ cup boiling water

¼ cup brown sugar

2 tablespoons honey

3 eggs

1 teaspoon vanilla essence

2 x 250g packets Kraft Philadelphia Cream Cheese

TOPPING

1 cup chopped dates

1 cup toasted walnuts

½ cup honey

Crush biscuits until fine crumbs. Melt butter and mix into biscuits. Press into the base of a baking-paper-lined 20cm loose-bottom cake tin. Pour in filling. Bake at 180°C for 1 hour. Cool then pour over topping.

FILLING

Place dates, water, sugar and honey in a bowl. Leave until cool. Place date mixture, eggs and vanilla in the bowl of a food processor with cream cheese. Process until cream cheese is mixed in.

TOPPING

Mix dates, walnuts and honey together until combined.

Serves 8 to 10.

Walnut and Date Cheesecake (top) and American Pumpkin and Pinenut Cheesecake

AMERICAN PUMPKIN AND PINENUT CHEESECAKE

250g packet vanilla wine biscuits

¼ cup pinenuts

100g butter

½ cup pinenuts

¼ cup honey

FILLING

250g packet Kraft Philadelphia Cream Cheese

½ cup sugar

2 cups cooked, drained, mashed pumpkin

1 teaspoon grated lemon rind

2 tablespoons lemon juice

1 teaspoon ground nutmeg

3 eggs

½ cup cream

Process biscuits and first measure of pinenuts in the bowl of a food processor until fine crumbs. Melt butter and mix in. Spread mixture into the base of a 20cm springform baking tin. Pour in filling. Sprinkle over second measure of pinenuts. Bake at 160°C for 1½ hours or until an inserted skewer comes out clean. Melt honey and brush over cheesecake. Serve at room temperature with pumpkin cream sauce.

FILLING

Soften cream cheese (see page 2) and beat with sugar until smooth. Mix in pumpkin, lemon rind, juice and nutmeg until combined. Separate eggs. Beat egg yolks into mixture. Beat egg whites until stiff. Whip cream until soft peaks form. Fold egg whites and cream into pumpkin mixture.

PUMPKIN CREAM SAUCE

150ml cream

½ cup cooked, drained, mashed pumpkin

1 tablespoon icing sugar

¼ teaspoon ground nutmeg

Whip cream until soft peaks form. Fold in pumpkin, icing sugar and nutmeg.

Serves 6 to 8.

CHILLED TROPICAL CHEESECAKE

125g coconut biscuits
50g butter
2 passionfruit
FILLING
440g can crushed pineapple
1 tablespoon gelatin
250g pot Kraft Soft Philadelphia Spreadable Cream Cheese
250g pot cottage cheese
1/2 cup coconut cream
1/4 cup sugar
1/4 cup passionfruit pulp
1 1/2 cups cream

Crush biscuits until fine crumbs. Melt butter and mix into biscuit crumbs. Press into the base of a 20cm round springform tin. Refrigerate while preparing filling. Pour filling into tin and refrigerate until set. Decorate with remaining cream and pulp from passionfruit.

FILLING

Drain pineapple, reserving 1 cup of juice. Pour juice into a saucepan. Sprinkle over gelatin and leave for 5 minutes to soften and swell. Heat until gelatin has dissolved. Cool then refrigerate until the consistency of raw egg white. Beat cream cheese with cottage cheese, coconut cream and sugar until creamy. Mix in partially set pineapple juice, pineapple and passionfruit pulp. Beat cream until soft peaks form. Fold half of the cream into the pineapple mixture.

Serves 6 to 8.

BAKED CHERRY CHEESECAKE

250g packet chocolate chip biscuits
75g butter
FILLING
250g packet Kraft Philadelphia Cream Cheese
1/4 cup cream
1 egg
1 egg yolk
1/4 cup sugar
425g can pitted cherries
1 teaspoon almond essence

Crush biscuits until fine crumbs. Melt butter. Mix crumbs and butter together and line the base and sides of a 20cm round springform tin with the crumb mixture. Bake at 160°C for 10 minutes or until firm. Pour in filling and bake at 160°C for 40 minutes or until filling is set. Serve with sweetened sour cream and fresh cherries if available.

FILLING

Soften cream cheese (see page 2). Gradually beat in cream. Beat egg, egg yolk and sugar together. Mix into cream cheese mixture with cherries and almond essence.

Serves 6 to 8.

Chilled Tropical Cheesecake and Baked Cherry Cheesecake

Quick'n'Easy

LIME CHEESECAKE

125g vanilla wine biscuits

50g butter

1 lime

1 cup water

1/2 cup sugar

FILLING

2 x 250g pots Kraft Light Philadelphia
    Spreadable Cream Cheese

1/2 cup sugar

1 tablespoon grated lime rind

1/4 cup lime juice

150ml cream

1 tablespoon gelatin

1/4 cup water

3 egg whites

Crush biscuits until fine crumbs.
Melt butter and mix with biscuit
crumbs until combined. Press into the
base of a 20cm round springform tin.
Chill while preparing the filling.
Pour in filling and refrigerate until set.
Cut lime into thin slices. Heat water
and sugar until boiling. Add lime
slices and simmer for 10 minutes or
until transparent. Drain and use to
decorate cheesecake.

FILLING

Beat cream cheese, sugar, lime rind
and juice together until smooth. Beat
in cream. Sprinkle gelatin over water
and leave for 5 minutes to soften and
swell. Heat over hot water until
dissolved. Beat into cream cheese
mixture. Beat egg whites until stiff
peaks form. Fold a little of the cream
cheese mixture into whites, then fold
into cream cheese mixture.

Serves 8 to 10.

STRAWBERRY SHORTCAKE CHEESECAKE

Make strawberry purée by hulling
strawberries and puréeing in a food
processor or blender. If you don't have
either of these appliances, mash
strawberries with a potato masher
until pulpy.

2 sheets sweet short pastry

250g pot Kraft Soft Philadelphia
    Spreadable Cream Cheese

1/2 cup low-fat sour cream

1/2 cup icing sugar

1 tablespoon gelatin

1/4 cup water

1/2 cup strawberry purée

10 strawberries

100g white chocolate

Cut a 20cm diameter circle from
one pastry sheet. Fit into the bottom
of a 20cm diameter springform or
loose-bottom cake tin. Bake at 190°C
for 10 to 15 minutes or until golden
and cooked. Cut small pastry shapes
from second pastry sheet and bake at
190°C for 10 minutes or until lightly
golden. Beat cream cheese with sour
cream and icing sugar. Sprinkle gelatin
over cold water and leave to soften for
5 minutes. Dissolve over hot water.
Mix into cream cheese mixture. Swirl
through strawberry purée. Pour into
cooked base. Refrigerate until set.
To serve, dip unhulled strawberries in
melted white chocolate and arrange on
cheesecake with pastry shapes.

Serves 6 to 8.

*Christmas Mincemeat Cheesecake,
Lime Cheesecake and
Strawberry Shortcake
Cheesecake*

CHRISTMAS MINCEMEAT CHEESECAKE

250g packet digestive biscuits

75g butter

2 tablespoons icing sugar

FILLING

250g packet Kraft Philadelphia
   Cream Cheese

4 eggs

250g pot plain cottage cheese

½ cup sugar

¼ cup cornflour

1 cup Christmas mincemeat

Crush biscuits until coarse crumbs.
Melt butter and mix into crumbs.
Press over the base of a 20cm round
springform tin. Pour in filling. Bake at
200°C for 10 minutes then reduce
heat to 180°C and cook for a further
35 to 40 minutes or until set. Leave to
cool in tin, then remove carefully.
Serve warm or at room temperature,
dusted with icing sugar.

FILLING

Soften cream cheese (see page 2).
Separate eggs. Beat cream cheese,
cottage cheese, sugar, cornflour and
egg yolks together until smooth.
Beat egg whites until stiff.
Fold cheese mixture into egg whites
with mincemeat.

Serves 8 to 10.

23

FROZEN APRICOT CHEESECAKE

Leave this to stand out of the freezer for 10 minutes before attempting to cut it.

250g packet vanilla wine biscuits

75g butter

FILLING

415g can SPC Apricots in Natural Juice

250g packet Kraft Philadelphia Cream Cheese

2 tablespoons sherry

150ml cream

SAUCE

415g can SPC Apricots in Natural Juice

2 tablespoons cornflour

Crush biscuits until fine crumbs. Melt butter and mix into biscuit crumbs. Press into the base of a 20cm square loose-bottom cake tin. Pour in filling and freeze until firm. To serve, cut into squares and pour over apricot sauce.

FILLING

Purée apricots and juice in a blender or food processor. Soften cream cheese (see page 2) and gradually work in the apricot mixture and sherry. Whip cream until soft peaks form. Fold into cream cheese mixture.

SAUCE

Purée apricots and juice in a blender or food processor. Mix a little of the purée to a smooth paste with the cornflour. Mix into apricot purée and heat, stirring, until the mixture boils and thickens.

Serves 8 to 10.

NEW YORK CHEESECAKE

12 digestive biscuits

$^1/_2$ cup blanched almonds

$^1/_4$ cup sugar

50g butter

FILLING

3 x 250g packets Kraft Philadelphia Cream Cheese

$^1/_2$ cup sugar

1 tablespoon lemon juice

2 teaspoons grated lemon rind

4 eggs

Place biscuits, almonds and sugar in the bowl of a food processor and process until fine crumbs. Alternatively crush biscuits and finely chop almonds. Melt butter and mix into crumb mixture. Press into the base of a 20cm springform tin. Pour in filling. Bake at 160°C for 55 to 60 minutes or until set. Cool and serve with fruit.

FILLING

Soften cream cheese (see page 2). Beat cream cheese, sugar, lemon juice, rind and eggs together until well combined.

Serves 8 to 10.

Quick Lemon Jelly Cheesecake (top left), Frozen Apricot Cheesecake and New York Cheesecake

QUICK LEMON JELLY CHEESECAKE

250g packet coconut biscuits

75g butter

Whipped cream

Lemon slices

FILLING

85g packet lemon jelly

250g pot Kraft Light Philadelphia
*   Spreadable Cream Cheese*

1 teaspoon grated lemon rind

2 egg whites

Crush biscuits until fine crumbs. Melt butter and mix into biscuits until combined. Press into the base and sides of a 20cm round springform tin. Use a glass to smooth base and sides. Pour in filling and refrigerate until set. Serve garnished with whipped cream and lemon slices.

FILLING

Make jelly to packet directions using only 250ml water. Leave until the consistency of raw egg white. Using an electric mixer, beat cream cheese and lemon rind into partially set jelly. Beat egg whites until stiff and fold cream cheese mixture into them.

Serves 6 to 8.

25

Quick 'n' Easy
TRADITIONAL FAVOURITES

*No dessert book would be complete without
acknowledging the origins of many desserts that
influence our sweet cuisine.*

*These desserts can usually be found in some modified form
in many cuisines, thereby reinforcing the importance of
a few basic ingredients and concepts in the
evolution of our food.*

*Some of these traditional favourites were quick to
prepare anyway, while others I have changed to be
true to the Quick 'n' Easy claim for this book.*

LINDA'S LEMON MERINGUE PIE

I'm very particular about my lemons and prefer those with a light skin and flesh and a tart lemon flavour. These are best for this pie.

400g sweet short pastry

$^1/_2$ cup custard powder

1 cup sugar

4 teaspoons grated lemon rind

1 cup lemon juice

1 cup water

50g butter

6 egg yolks

MERINGUE

4 egg whites

$^3/_4$ cup sugar

Roll pastry out on a lightly floured board to a 4mm thickness and use to line the base and sides of a 24cm pie dish, shallow cake tin or flan dish. Bake blind at 190°C for 20 minutes. Remove baking blind material and return to oven for 5 minutes to dry out base. Mix custard powder, sugar, lemon rind and juice together in a saucepan until smooth. Mix in water. Cook over a medium heat until mixture boils and thickens, stirring constantly. Remove from heat and mix in butter and egg yolks. Return to a low heat and cook for 1 minute, stirring constantly. Pour filling into pastry shell. Cover with meringue and bake at 190°C for 10 minutes or until lightly golden.

MERINGUE

Beat egg whites and sugar together until thick and glossy.

Serves 6 to 8.

Linda's Lemon Meringue Pie

NO STODGE CHRISTMAS PUDDING

Save the crumbs in the bottom of the Weet-bix packet to make this delicious light Christmas pudding. Use whatever combination of dried fruit you prefer.

125g butter

2 tablespoons golden syrup

1 teaspoon baking soda

1 cup grated carrot

2 cups crushed Weet-bix

³/₄ cup wholemeal flour

¹/₂ cup brown sugar

2 cups mixed dried fruit

2 teaspoons mixed spice

1 teaspoon cinnamon

1 egg

¹/₂ cup milk or brandy

2 teaspoons vanilla essence

Melt butter and golden syrup in a saucepan large enough to mix all the ingredients. Remove from heat and mix in baking soda. Add carrot, Weet-bix, flour, brown sugar, dried fruit, spices, egg, milk and vanilla. Mix with a wooden spoon until combined. Spoon mixture into a greased six-cup capacity pudding basin. Cover with a layer of baking paper and foil. Secure with string, making a handle across the basin to lift pudding into and out of the saucepan. Place an old inverted saucer or trivet in a saucepan of boiling water. Cover and steam for 3 hours. Remove from saucepan and serve, or reheat in the same way for 1 hour or in the microwave on 50% power for 12 to 15 minutes. Stand covered for 5 minutes. Serve hot with brandy sauce.

Serves 8 to 10.

APRICOT STEAMED PUDDING

Steamed puddings are part of our culinary heritage so here's a more modern slant on this traditional favourite.

415g can SPC Apricot Halves in Natural Juice
1 teaspoon grated orange rind
100g butter
$1/2$ cup sugar
1 egg
$1^1/_4$ cups flour
2 teaspoons baking powder
About $1/2$ cup orange juice
$1/4$ cup brown sugar
1 tablespoon cornflour

Drain apricots, reserving juice. Chop apricots and mix with half a cup of the reserved juice and the orange rind. Melt butter in a saucepan large enough to mix all the ingredients. Remove from heat and add sugar and egg. Mix well. Sift in flour and baking powder and mix in with apricot mixture until combined. Spoon into a greased six-cup capacity pudding basin. Make remaining reserved juice up to one cup with orange juice. Mix brown sugar and cornflour together and sprinkle over pudding. Pour juice mixture over pudding over the back of a spoon. Cover pudding with a layer of baking paper and foil. Secure with string, making a string handle to lift pudding into and out of a saucepan of boiling water. The water should come half-way up the sides of the pudding basin. Cover and simmer for 2 hours, topping up water during cooking as necessary. To serve, turn pudding onto a plate so sauce flows over pudding. Serve hot.

Serves 4 to 6.

No Stodge Christmas Pudding and Apricot Steamed Pudding

LUSCIOUS BREAD AND BUTTER PUDDING

2 tablespoons butter

5 slices stale bread

500ml low-fat cream

4 eggs

$^1/_2$ cup sugar

1 teaspoon vanilla essence

415g can SPC 100% Apricot

Icing sugar

Butter bread, remove crusts and arrange in a 23 x 18cm ovenproof dish. Heat cream to boiling point but do not boil. Beat eggs, sugar and vanilla together until combined. Pour cream into eggs, mixing well. Purée 100% Apricot in a blender or processor. Spoon dollops over bread. Pour over egg mixture. Place dish in a roasting dish. Place in oven and pour water into the oven dish to come three-quarters of the way up the sides of the dish. Bake at 160°C for 45 to 50 minutes or until pudding is set. Serve warm dusted with icing sugar.

Serves 4 to 6.

CREAMY RICE PUDDING

This is so simple to make but time-consuming to cook. If you can manage the cooking time the result is well worth it. Use whatever milk type you prefer. Some of the calcium-enriched non-fat varieties do tend to curdle.

$^1/_4$ cup short grain rice

3 tablespoons sugar

$^1/_4$ teaspoon salt

3 cups milk

1 teaspoon vanilla essence

$^1/_4$ teaspoon ground nutmeg

25g butter

415g can SPC Peach Slices in Light Syrup

Place rice in a four-cup capacity ovenproof dish. Mix sugar, salt, milk, vanilla and nutmeg together. Pour over rice. Dot butter over. Bake uncovered at 150°C for 2 hours or until rice is thick and creamy. Stir twice during first hour of cooking. Serve hot with peaches.

Serves 4.

Luscious Bread and Butter Pudding and Creamy Rice Pudding

APPLE CRUMBLE

Add sultanas or raisins and whole cloves to this for a strudel approach.

2 x 415g cans SPC 100% Apple

1 teaspoon grated lemon rind

50g butter

1/2 cup flour

1/2 cup brown sugar

1/2 cup rolled oats

Place apples in a 22 x 18cm ovenproof dish. Mix through lemon rind. Melt butter. Mix flour, brown sugar and rolled oats together. Pour in butter and mix through. Sprinkle over apple and press down. Bake at 190°C for 30 minutes or until golden and crisp.

Serves 4 to 6.

TRIFLE

This is also part of our British-based culinary heritage but with a faster approach than our grandmothers were able to enjoy. Use readymade custard for this recipe or make your own if preferred.

140g piece stale sponge cake

1/2 cup raspberry jam

1/2 cup gingerale or sherry

415g can SPC Peach Slices in Light Syrup

600ml prepared custard

300ml whipped cream

1/4 cup chopped walnuts

Spread one side of sponge with jam and cut into 2cm cubes. Arrange jammed sponge in a serving bowl. Sprinkle with gingerale or sherry. Drain peach slices. Reserve a few for garnish. Arrange remaining peaches over the sponge. Pour over custard, pushing a knife down into sponge to let custard soak through. Spread trifle with cream and decorate with walnuts and reserved peach slices. Chill until ready to serve.

Serves 6 to 8.

Trifle and Apple Crumble

PAVLOVA'S PAVLOVA

Rivalry between Australia and New Zealand makes it hard to risk claiming the origins of this dessert. We do know that it evolved as a tribute to the ballerina Pavlova during a visit to both countries many years ago. Here's a foolproof recipe that requires an electric mixer for ease and success. I use a cake tin to mark my 20cm circle.

4 egg whites

1¼ cups sugar

1 teaspoon vinegar

1 teaspoon vanilla essence

1 tablespoon cornflour

1 cup whipped cream

SPC canned fruit or fresh seasonal fruit or a mixture of both

Preheat oven to 180°C. Beat egg whites and sugar in a clean mixer bowl on maximum speed for 10 minutes or until thick, and stiff peaks form. Mix vinegar, vanilla and cornflour together. Beat into egg white mixture and continue beating for a further 4 minutes or until mixture is thick and glossy. Place a sheet of baking paper on an oven tray and mark out a 20cm diameter circle. Spoon pavlova mixture to within 2cm from circle edge. Place pavlova in preheated oven then reduce oven temperature to 100°C. Bake for 1 hour. Turn oven off and leave pavlova to cool in oven. To serve, cover with whipped cream and decorate with drained and prepared fruit.

Serves 6 to 8.

PAVLOVA ROLL

This is an alternative way to cook a pavlova mixture.

Spread mixture into a baking-paper-lined 20 x 30cm sponge roll tin. Bake at 180°C for 15 to 20 minutes or until golden and set. Turn pavlova onto an icing sugar dusted piece of baking paper. Remove paper base and leave to cool for 5 to 10 minutes. Fill with whipped cream and fruit. Roll in from the long side using baking paper to help. Chill and serve sliced.

Serves 6 to 8.

APPLE PIE

Traditional favourites have to be modified to suit the times and ingredients available. Here's a pie that is every bit as good as those made from scratch. These sorts of pies cook better in a metal pie dish. If using a ceramic dish, increase the heat to 200 to 210°C.

400g packet sweet short pastry

2 x 415g cans SPC 100% Apple

8 whole cloves or ¹/₂ teaspoon ground cloves

2 teaspoons milk

2 tablespoons caster sugar

Cut one-third from the pastry and set aside. Roll larger piece out on a lightly floured board and use to line the base of a 24cm pie dish. Spread apple in pastry shell. Press cloves into apple or gently mix through ground cloves. Roll remaining pastry out to make a pastry lid. Wet pastry edges and press lid on, sealing edges. Trim pastry by running a knife around the edge of the dish. Brush pastry top with milk, sprinkle with sugar and make two steam holes in the centre. Bake at 190°C for 45 minutes or until pastry is lightly golden. Serve hot or cold.

Serves 4 to 6.

From top clockwise: Apple Pie, Pavlova Roll, Pavlova's Pavlova and Crème Caramel

CREME CARAMEL

This has to be one of the easiest and most enjoyable puds for custard lovers. For extra ease and speed a half cup of golden syrup or maple syrup can be used on the bottom of the dish instead of caramelising the sugar.

CARAMEL

1 cup sugar

1 cup water

CUSTARD

3 eggs

3 egg yolks

¹/₄ cup sugar

3 cups milk

CARAMEL

Place sugar and water in a frying pan. Stir to dissolve over a low heat then boil rapidly, without stirring, until caramel is a light golden colour. Quickly pour caramel into a dry 20cm ovenproof dish or six individual dishes. Pour custard mixture through a sieve over caramel. Cover with foil, place dish in a roasting dish and pour water into roasting dish to come half-way up the sides of the custard dish. Bake at 160°C for 40 to 50 minutes or until custard is set. For individual dishes, bake in the same way for 30 minutes. To test for setting, an inserted knife should come out clean. Cool before turning onto a serving plate.

CUSTARD

Lightly beat eggs, yolks and sugar together until combined but not frothy. Mix in milk.

Serves 6.

33

Quick 'n' Easy
COLD DESSERTS

When fruit is used as the basic ingredient, there are

so many cold dessert choices.

Often when we are presented with numerous choices

we end up being overwhelmed and do nothing.

So a few standard useful recipes to have in your cold dessert

repertoire are what is needed to ensure you can always turn

your hand to a quick and easy dessert to enjoy anytime.

So Easy Chocolate Pots

Add a tablespoon of liqueur to this mixture for a different flavour.

200g cooking chocolate

3 eggs

2 teaspoons vanilla essence

1 tablespoon gelatin

¹/₂ cup boiling water

Chocolate sticks

Break or chop chocolate into pieces. Place in the bowl of a food processor or blender with the eggs, vanilla, gelatin and water. Process or blend until smooth. Pour into individual serving dishes or a serving bowl and refrigerate until set. Garnish with chocolate sticks.

Serves 4 to 6.

Peaches and Cream Iced Terrine

2 x 415g cans SPC Peach Slices in Natural Juice

300ml prepared vanilla custard

2 litres vanilla ice cream

1 tablespoon custard powder

Drain peaches, reserving juice. Purée one can of slices in a blender or food processor. Mix whole peach slices and custard together. Soften ice cream and beat in custard mixture. Spread mixture into two 19 x 10cm loaf tins. Pour over peach purée and swirl through icc cream with a knife. Freeze until firm. Mix reserved juice and custard powder together. Bring to the boil, stirring constantly until mixture boils and thickens. Remove from heat and place a piece of plastic wrap over the surface of the sauce to prevent a skin forming. Turn terrine onto a serving plate. Serve sliced with peach sauce.

Serves 10 to 12.

So Easy Chocolate Pots and Peaches and Cream Iced Terrine

QUICK FIX APRICOTS IN MULLED WINE

1 lemon

1 cup sweet white wine such as sauterne

$^1\!/_2$ cup sugar

1 cinnamon stick

6 whole cloves

2 x 415g cans SPC Lite Apricot Halves

Thinly pare rind from lemon and cut into thin strips. Mix lemon rind, wine, sugar, cinnamon stick and cloves together in a saucepan. Bring to the boil and simmer for 5 minutes. Remove from heat. Drain apricots and add to wine syrup. Leave to marinate in syrup. When cool enough, refrigerate. Serve chilled with whipped cream.

Serves 4 to 6.

PEACH MELBA SUSHI

Toast coconut in a frying pan over a medium heat, tossing until it starts to change colour. Remove pan from heat and toss coconut until lightly golden.

1 cup short grain rice

400g can coconut cream

$^1\!/_2$ cup sugar

1 cup toasted coconut

$^1\!/_4$ cup sugar

415g can SPC Lite Peach Slices

4 sheets nori

Prepared raspberry sauce

Cook rice, coconut cream and first measure of sugar over a medium heat for 35 minutes or until creamy. Spread rice mixture out onto a piece of aluminium foil to cool. Mix coconut and second measure of sugar together. Drain peaches and cut in half lengthwise. Place nori on a board or sushi mat. Spread about half a cup of rice mixture over nori. Sprinkle over quarter of a cup of coconut mixture and arrange a row of peach slices down the centre. Roll up, using a sushi mat or tea towel to help, as you would for a sponge roll. Press roll together to seal edges. Chill until ready to serve. Cut sweet sushi into 2cm pieces on the diagonal. Serve with raspberry sauce.

Serves 8 to 10.

Peach Melba Sushi and
Quick Fix Apricots in Mulled Wine

SUMMER PUDDING

Use any berry mixture for this dessert.

6 cups mixed raspberries, blackberries, boysenberries, strawberries

1 cup sugar

15 slices stale bread

Prepare fruit as necessary. Mix fruit and sugar together and heat until almost boiling. Cool. Cut crusts from bread. Arrange bread slightly overlapping around the inside of a six-cup capacity non-metal pudding basin. Spoon one-third of berry mixture into bread-lined basin. Layer with more bread. Repeat, finishing with a layer of bread. Spoon over enough berry juice to moisten bread. Cover with plastic wrap and place something heavy on top. Cans of fruit are good for this. Refrigerate for 2 hours or overnight. To serve, turn onto a serving plate and cut into slices. Serve with softly whipped cream.

Serves 6 to 8.

NAPOLEON SLICE

2 sheets flaky puff pastry

225g can crushed pineapple

2 tablespoons gelatin

600ml cream

¼ cup icing sugar

2 teaspoons grated lemon rind

1 egg white

Icing sugar

Prick pastry sheets with a fork. Place on a baking tray and bake at 210°C for 10 minutes or until golden. Cool. Drain pineapple, reserving juice. Sprinkle gelatin over juice and leave to swell for 5 minutes. Heat over hot water until gelatin dissolves. Beat cream until soft peaks form. Fold pineapple, icing sugar, gelatin and lemon rind into cream. Refrigerate for 10 minutes or until the consistency of raw egg white. Beat egg white until stiff. Fold a little cream mixture into egg white then fold mixtures together. Spread mixture over one pastry sheet. Top with another sheet. Refrigerate until firm. To serve cut into slices and sprinkle with icing sugar.

Serves 8 to 10.

Summer Pudding and Napoleon Slice

SORBET FRUIT PLATTER

APRICOT SORBET

415g can SPC Apricot Halves
   in Natural Juice

¹/₄ teaspoon almond essence

1 egg white

PEAR AND COCONUT GRANITA

415g can SPC Pear Halves
   in Natural Juice

¹/₄ cup coconut cream

2 tablespoons lemon juice

1 egg white

TO SERVE

Fresh fruit or canned SPC fruit

APRICOT SORBET

Place undrained apricots in the bowl of a food processor or blender. Process or blend until smooth. Mix in essence. Freeze until slushy. Remove from freezer. Beat egg white until stiff and fold slush into white. Refreeze until ready to serve.

PEAR AND COCONUT GRANITA

Purée undrained pears with coconut cream and lemon juice. Freeze until slushy. Beat egg white until stiff. Fold fruit mixture into egg white until combined. Refreeze until ready to serve.

TO SERVE

Arrange fresh or drained canned fruit on individual dishes with a scoop of sorbet and a shaving of granita.

Serves 4 to 6.

*Spectacular Strawberry
Ice Cream Roll and
Chocolate Pâté with
Sorbet Fruit Platter*

SPECTACULAR STRAWBERRY ICE CREAM ROLL

2 litres vanilla ice cream

2 teaspoons grated orange rind

¹/₄ cup orange marmalade

1 small chip strawberries

Soften ice cream and mix in orange rind and marmalade. Spread into a plastic-wrap-lined 20 x 30cm sponge roll tin. Freeze until firm. Hull strawberries. Cut half the strawberries into quarters. Arrange over the surface of the ice cream, pressing them into the surface gently. Remove ice cream from the tin and, using the plastic wrap as a guide, carefully roll ice cream up from the long side. Wrap in plastic wrap and refreeze. Purée remaining strawberries. Cut roll into slices and serve with strawberry purée.

Serves 8 to 10.

CHOCOLATE PATE

This is not the dessert to serve if you are watching your fat intake. It's a great way to use leftover egg yolks and makes a simple but chic dessert idea to end a meal.

500g cooking chocolate

100g butter

4 egg yolks

¹/₄ cup cream

Fresh fruit or SPC canned fruit

Biscotti

Melt chocolate and butter over a gentle heat. Mix in egg yolks until well combined. Remove from heat. Mix in cream. Line a 10 x 20cm loaf tin with baking paper to come over sides and bottom of tin. Pour mixture into prepared tin. Refrigerate until set. To serve, remove from tin and cut into slices. Serve with fresh fruit or drained and dried canned fruit and biscotti.

Serves 10.

Quick'n'Easy

IRISH CREAM POTS

Use Irish cream liqueur instead of coffee and brandy for this dessert if wished.

2 tablespoons instant coffee

2 tablespoons brandy

500ml prepared custard

300ml cream

2 egg whites

Chocolate shavings or coffee beans

Dissolve coffee in brandy. Mix into custard. Whip cream until stiff peaks form. Beat egg whites until stiff. Fold custard mixture and cream into egg whites. Spoon into individual serving dishes and refrigerate until ready to serve. Garnish with chocolate shavings or coffee beans.

Serves 6 to 8.

QUICK CHOCOLATE MOUSSE

150g cooking chocolate

4 eggs

300ml cream

3 tablespoons icing sugar

Fresh fruit

Break chocolate into a saucepan and melt over a gentle heat or over hot water. Separate eggs and mix yolks into melted chocolate. Beat until smooth. Beat cream until thick. Fold cream into chocolate mixture. Beat egg whites until stiff. Beat in icing sugar, beating until thick. Fold chocolate mixture into egg whites. Pour into individual serving dishes or one bowl. Chill until firm. Garnish with fresh fruit.

Serves 6 to 8.

From top clockwise:
Quick Chocolate Mousse,
Toastie Parfait,
Homemade Fruit Jelly
and Irish Cream Pots

HOMEMADE FRUIT JELLY

When you make your own jelly for the first time you will wonder why it took so long to discover such a delicious and simple dessert. Any fruit or juice can be used to make a jelly like this.

500g frozen raspberries

¼ cup sugar

1 tablespoon gelatin

2 tablespoons water

Thaw raspberries, reserving juice. Mix raspberries and juice with sugar in a saucepan and bring to the boil. Strain raspberries thoroughly, reserving juice. Soak gelatin in water for 5 minutes. Mix into hot juice until dissolved. Pour into a wet three-cup-capacity jelly mould or bowl. Refrigerate when cool. To unmould jelly when set, dip bowl or mould quickly into hot water and turn onto a serving plate, shaking hard to release the vacuum. Serve with fresh fruit and yoghurt.

Serves 4.

TOASTIE PARFAIT

1 cup soft brown breadcrumbs

1 cup brown sugar

½ cup rolled oats

½ cup chopped walnuts

415g can SPC Lite Peach Slices

1 litre prepared vanilla custard

Whipped cream

Place breadcrumbs, sugar, oats and walnuts in a roasting dish and bake at 200°C for 15 minutes or until lightly golden. Cool. Drain peaches. Layer peaches, custard and breadcrumb mixture in tall glasses. Finish with peaches or cream.

Serves 4.

STRAWBERRY PALMIERS WITH ORANGE CREAM

2 sheets prerolled flaky pastry

¼ cup sugar

1 teaspoon grated orange rind

6 large strawberries

125g Kraft Soft Philadelphia Spreadable Cream Cheese

2 tablespoons orange marmalade

Place pastry on an oven tray. Mix sugar and orange rind together and sprinkle over pastry sheets. Roll pastry in two rolls to the centre from one side and then from the other side to the centre. Cut into 0.5cm thick slices. Bake at 200°C for 10 minutes or until golden and cooked. Cool on a wire rack. Hull strawberries and halve. Mix cream cheese and marmalade together. Spread palmiers with cream cheese mixture, top with strawberries then top each palmier with another palmier, cream cheese side to the strawberries.

Makes 22.

CARAMELISED FRUIT SALAD PLATTER

8 cups prepared fresh fruit or SPC canned fruit, such as peaches, apricots, pears, kiwifruit, strawberries, raspberries

1 cup sugar

½ cup water

Whipped cream

Arrange fruit on a large platter. Dissolve sugar in water over a low heat. Increase heat and heat syrup without stirring until mixture is a light golden colour. Remove from heat and pour over fruit. Serve with whipped cream.

Serves 10 to 12.

Caramelised Fruit Platter and Strawberry Palmiers with Orange Cream

GINGER ICE CREAM BRULEES

1 litre French vanilla ice cream

1/4 cup chopped ginger in syrup

2 tablespoons ginger syrup

1 cup sugar

1/2 cup water

Soften ice cream. Mix drained ginger and the syrup into ice cream. Pack ice cream into 5 individual half-cup-capacity ramekins. Freeze until firm. Mix sugar and water together in a frying pan over a medium heat, stirring until sugar dissolves. Continue to heat without stirring until mixture starts to colour. When light golden, remove from heat and pour over ramekins. Stand for 5 to 10 minutes before serving.

Serves 5.

QUICK LEMON YOGHURT SOUFFLE

1/2 cup lemon juice

2 tablespoons gelatin

3 cups natural unsweetened yoghurt

2 teaspoons grated lemon rind

1/2 cup sugar

1 cup cream

3 egg whites

Strips of lemon rind

YOGHURT CREAM

1 cup natural sweetened yoghurt

1 cup whipped cream

Tie a paper collar around the outside of a four-cup-capacity soufflé dish to stand 5cm above the dish. Mix lemon juice and gelatin together and leave for 5 minutes to swell. Heat over hot water until gelatin is dissolved. Mix yoghurt, sugar and lemon rind together. Mix in gelatin mixture. Beat cream until stiff. Beat egg whites until stiff peaks form. Fold cream into yoghurt mixture. Fold yoghurt mixture into egg whites until combined. Pour into prepared dish and refrigerate until set. To serve, carefully remove paper collar. Garnish with strips of lemon rind and serve with yoghurt cream.

YOGHURT CREAM

Mix yoghurt and whipped cream together.

Quick Lemon Yoghurt Souffle and Ginger Ice Cream Brûlées

Serves 6 to 8.

Quick'n'Easy
HOT DESSERTS

A bleak winter's night when it's cold, windy and raining is

just the time we need a little comfort food in the

form of a warming, satisfying hot dessert.

I often think of these as hollow-leg fillers for appetites

with an edge from the winter cold.

Here are some ideas that will suit entertaining or

family meals when you need great taste

with minimum fuss.

GRILLED APRICOTS

*415g can SPC Apricot Halves in
    Natural Juice*

¼ cup brown sugar

10 amaretto biscuits

1 egg yolk

300ml cream

1 tablespoon icing sugar

½ teaspoon almond essence

Drain apricots, reserving juice. Place apricots cut side down in an ovenproof dish and grill until lightly golden. Turn apricots over. Sprinkle over brown sugar. Crush biscuits and mix with egg yolk. Measure teaspoonfuls of mixture and place in the stone cavity of the apricots. Pour over quarter of a cup of the reserved apricot juice. Bake at 180°C for 10 minutes. Whip cream until stiff. Mix in icing sugar and almond essence. Serve with hot apricots.

Serves 4.

SWEET PIROSHKIS

50g Kraft Philadelphia Cream Cheese

*415g can SPC Apricot Halves in
    Natural Juice*

3 sheets sweet short pastry

415g can SPC 100% Apricot

2 tablespoons water

Icing sugar

2 tablespoons cream

CARAMEL CHOCOLATE SAUCE

25g butter

1 cup brown sugar

1 cup cream

75g cooking chocolate

Cut cream cheese into 1cm cubes. Drain apricots, reserving juice, and cut apricots in half. Cut 11cm rounds from pastry. Place a cream cheese cube and an apricot half in the centre of the pastry rounds. Wrap pastry around filling. Place join side down on a baking-paper-lined oven tray. Bake at 200°C for 15 minutes or until pastry is lightly golden. Purée 100% Apricot with water. Stack piroshkis on a plate in a cone shape. Dust with icing sugar. Pour over apricot purée and Caramel Chocolate Sauce. Serve immediately.

CARAMEL CHOCOLATE SAUCE

Melt butter and sugar in a small saucepan. Add cream. Bring to boil, stirring. Remove from heat, stir in chocolate until melted.

Serves 6 to 8.

*Sweet Piroshkis
and Grilled
Apricots*

Caramel Brownie with Chocolate Bar Sauce

250g butter

½ cup golden syrup

1 cup brown sugar

4 eggs

1 teaspoon baking soda

1¼ cups flour

2 teaspoons vanilla essence

1 Moro or Mars bar

2 tablespoons cream

Melt butter, golden syrup and brown sugar in a saucepan large enough to mix all the ingredients. Cool slightly. Beat in eggs with a wooden spoon. Beat in baking soda. Sift flour into mixture and mix in with vanilla essence. Pour mixture into a baking-paper-lined 20 x 30cm sponge roll tin. Bake at 180°C for 25 to 30 minutes or until brownie springs back when lightly touched. Roughly chop chocolate bar. Place in a saucepan and heat gently with the cream until melted. Spread over brownie. Cool before cutting.

Serves 8 to 10.

Caramelised Pears

1 sheet flaky pastry

415g can SPC Pear Halves in Natural Juice

50g butter

3 tablespoons brown sugar

300ml cream

1 tablespoon golden syrup

Cut pastry sheet in half. Cut each half into four rectangles. Cut the four rectangles on the diagonal. Place on an oven tray. Bake at 200°C for 10 minutes or until golden and cooked. Drain pears. Melt butter. Add brown sugar and heat until bubbling. Add pears and cook gently for 3 to 4 minutes, carefully turning pears to coat in caramel mixture. Arrange pears on a pastry rectangle, drizzling over a little caramel mixture. Whip cream and mix in golden syrup. Spoon over hot pears and arrange pastry triangles with pears. Serve immediately.

Serves 6.

Café Date Pudding with Date Sauce

1½ cups dates

1 teaspoon baking soda

½ cup boiling water

150g butter

¾ cup brown sugar

2 eggs

1½ cups flour

2 teaspoons baking powder

DATE SAUCE

1 cup dates

1 cup orange juice

¼ cup brown sugar

1 cup cream

Roughly chop dates. Sprinkle over baking soda. Pour over boiling water. Set aside while preparing remaining ingredients. Melt butter and brown sugar in a saucepan large enough to mix all the ingredients. Remove from heat and cool slightly. Add eggs and beat with a wooden spoon to combine. Sift flour and baking powder into mixture and beat to combine. Pour mixture into a baking-paper-lined 20cm square cake tin. Bake at 180°C for 40 to 45 minutes or until cake springs back when lightly touched. Serve warm with date sauce.

DATE SAUCE

Chop dates finely. Place in a saucepan with orange juice and brown sugar. Bring to the boil and cook for 5 minutes or until pulpy. Remove from heat. Cool slightly then mix in cream.

Serves 10 to 12.

Caramel Brownie,
Café Date Pudding with Date Sauce,
and Caramelised Pears

GULLIBLE PUDDING

This is for my children who were going through a stage of resisting new foods when I served this pudding. I had to tell them it was something else and when they tasted it they realised they had been tricked, hence the gullible tag.

415g can SPC 100% Apple

1 cup flour

1 teaspoon baking powder

¹/₂ cup rolled oats

100g butter

¹/₂ cup brown sugar

1 tablespoon cornflour

¹/₄ cup boiling water

Place apple in an ovenproof dish. Mix flour, baking powder and rolled oats together. Melt butter and mix through flour mixture. Sprinkle over apple. Mix brown sugar and cornflour together. Sprinkle over flour mixture. Pour boiling water over the back of a spoon onto the pudding. Bake at 180°C for 25 minutes or until crusty on top. Serve hot with custard.

Serves 4.

*Quick Apple Strudel,
Tropical Clafouti and
Gullible Pudding*

QUICK APPLE STRUDEL

6 sheets filo pastry

¹/₂ cup soft breadcrumbs

2 x 415g cans SPC 100% Apple

¹/₂ cup sultanas

¹/₂ teaspoon ground cloves

¹/₂ teaspoon mixed spice

1 tablespoon melted butter

1 teaspoon icing sugar

Lay pastry sheets under a damp tea-towel, sprinkling breadcrumbs between each sheet. Mix apple, sultanas, cloves and mixed spice together. Spread apple mixture down centre of pastry to within 3cm of ends. Roll one long end of pastry layer over filling and roll as for a sponge roll. Place on a baking tray. Mix melted butter and icing sugar together. Brush around edges of pastry. Fold in short ends over filling. Roll from long side as for a sponge roll. Place on a baking tray. Brush with remaining butter mixture. Slash strudel top. Bake at 200°C for 20 to 25 minutes or until pastry is lightly golden and cooked. Serve warm.

Serves 8 to 10.

TROPICAL CLAFOUTI

*250g pot Kraft Soft Philadelphia
  Spreadable Cream Cheese*

3 eggs

¹/₂ cup sugar

¹/₂ cup custard powder

*432g can crushed pineapple in
  natural juice*

2 teaspoons grated lemon rind

¹/₄ cup passionfruit pulp

¹/₄ cup coconut

Place cream cheese in the bowl of a food processor or blender with eggs, sugar, custard powder, crushed pineapple and lemon rind. Process or blend until well combined. Add passionfruit pulp and mix in quickly so as not to crush seeds. Pour into a greased 20cm quiche dish. Sprinkle over coconut. Bake at 180°C for 30 to 40 minutes or until set. Serve warm.

Serves 6 to 8.

Orange and Peach French Toast

4 slices stale toast bread

2 eggs

1 teaspoon grated orange rind

2 tablespoons orange juice

50g butter

415g can SPC Peach Slices in Light Syrup

Icing sugar

Cut crusts from bread. Cut bread in half diagonally. Lightly beat eggs, orange rind and juice together in a shallow dish. Dip bread in this to soak. Melt butter in a frying pan and cook soaked bread over a medium heat until golden. Drain on absorbent paper. Add drained peaches to pan and cook quickly for 2 minutes or until heated through. Arrange on top of French toast, allowing one slice of bread per serving. Dust with icing sugar and serve with yoghurt.

Serves 4.

Apple Fritters

Don't beat egg whites too far in advance. They will separate irretrievably.

1 cup flour

$^1/_4$ cup cornflour

$^1/_2$ teaspoon baking powder

2 eggs

$^1/_2$ cup milk

415g can SPC 100% Apple

Oil or butter for shallow frying

Caster sugar

Lemon wedges

Sift flour, cornflour and baking powder into a bowl. Separate eggs. Beat yolks and milk together. Beat egg whites until stiff. Mix milk mixture and apple into flour then fold in egg whites. Cook quarter cupsful in hot oil until golden. Serve hot, dusted with sugar and garnished with lemon wedges.

Serves 6 to 8.

*Apple Fritters and
Orange and Peach French Toast*

Hot Fruit Salad with Biscuit Curls

415g can SPC Apricot Halves in Natural Juice

415g can SPC Pear Halves in Natural Juice

$^1/_2$ cup pitted dates

$^1/_2$ cup pitted prunes

2 tablespoons brown sugar

1 teaspoon grated orange rind

$^1/_4$ cup orange juice

1 banana

8 coconut biscuits

Drain apricot and pear juice into a saucepan. Set apricots and pears aside. Heat juices and add dates, prunes and brown sugar. Bring to boil and simmer for 10 minutes. Remove from heat and stir in orange rind and juice. Peel banana and slice into hot syrup. Cut pears into quarters and add with apricots to saucepan. Bring to the boil then pour into a heatproof serving bowl. Soften coconut biscuits at 180°C for 5 minutes. Remove from oven. Roll with a rolling pin or bottle to flatten then carefully mould around a wooden spoon handle. Leave to cool. Serve with hot fruit salad.

Serves 8.

Chocolate SSP

This is the ever-popular self-saucing pudding.

50g butter

1 cup flour

2 teaspoons baking powder

2 tablespoons cocoa

$^1/_2$ cup sugar

$^1/_2$ cup milk

1 teaspoon vanilla essence

$^1/_2$ cup brown sugar

1 tablespoon cocoa

$1^1/_2$ cups boiling water

Icing sugar

Melt butter in a saucepan large enough to mix all the ingredients. Sift flour, baking powder and first measure of cocoa into butter. Add sugar, milk and vanilla essence and beat with a wooden spoon until combined. Pour into a greased four-cup ovenproof dish. Mix brown sugar and second measure of cocoa together. Sprinkle over batter in dish. Pour boiling water over the back of a spoon onto the surface of the pudding. Bake at 180°C for 35 to 40 minutes or until pudding springs back when lightly touched. Dust with icing sugar.

Serves 4 to 6.

Chocolate SSP and Hot Fruit Salad with Biscuit Curls

Quick 'n' Easy
TARTS & PIES

Ever popular, sweet pies and tarts are something we don't

always choose to cook because we think of them as time-

consuming, with all that pastry making, rolling and trimming.

Thanks to prerolled pastry and packets of filo pastry, making a

"homemade" pie or tart is a breeze.

It takes many times longer to cook these yummies than it does to

prepare them, so impress your family and friends by including

these in your quick dessert repertoire.

Quick'n'Easy

STRAWBERRY SHORTCAKE

You can use this idea with virtually any berries, matching the jam to suit. Try a mixture of berries for a good look. It sure beats that boring bowl of strawberries we see served au natural every summer.

1 1/2 cups flour
1 teaspoon baking powder
1/4 cup icing sugar
150g butter
1 egg
250g pot Kraft Soft Philadelphia Spreadable Cream Cheese
1/4 cup icing sugar
1/2 cup strawberry jam
2 cups strawberries
1/2 cup sugar
1/2 cup water

Place flour, baking powder and icing sugar in the bowl of a food processor or a bowl. Mix to combine. Cut in butter until mixture resembles fine crumbs. Add egg and a little water if necessary to make a stiff dough. Make a 20cm circle on a baking-paper-covered oven tray. Press dough out to fill the circle. Bake at 190°C for 20 to 25 minutes. Cool. Mix cream cheese and icing sugar. Spread shortcake with cream cheese then spread over jam. Hull strawberries and cut in half if large. Arrange strawberries over shortcake. Heat sugar and water together over a medium heat, stirring until dissolved. Increase heat and cook sugar mixture until a light golden. Remove from heat. Cool slightly then pour over strawberries. Working quickly, use a fork to pull threads up from the caramel.

Serves 4 to 6.

Strawberry Shortcake

Maple Nut Pie

If your budget runs to it, use real maple syrup. Mine suits a maple flavoured syrup better.

400g packet sweet short pastry

3 eggs

25g butter

1 cup maple flavoured syrup

¼ cup brown sugar

2 tablespoons cornflour

2 teaspoons vanilla essence

1 cup roughly chopped walnuts or pecans

10 walnut or pecan halves

Roll pastry out on a lightly floured board and use to line a 20cm flan dish. Bake blind at 200°C for 10 minutes. Remove baking blind material and return pastry shell to oven for 4 minutes to dry out. Beat eggs until light and fluffy. Melt butter and add to eggs with syrup, brown sugar, cornflour and vanilla. Beat to combine. Mix in nuts and pour into cooked pastry shell. Arrange walnut or pecan halves over filling and bake at 150°C for 50 to 55 minutes or until filling is set. Serve warm or cold.

Serves 6 to 8.

Chocolate Cinnamon Pear Pie

2 cups flour

1 teaspoon cinnamon

2 tablespoons cocoa

2 tablespoons icing sugar

250g butter

¼ cup chocolate hazelnut spread

2 x 415g cans SPC Pears in Light Syrup

Mix flour, cinnamon, cocoa and icing sugar together in the bowl of a food processor or bowl until combined. Process or rub in butter until mixture resembles coarse crumbs. Roll half the pastry out on a lightly floured board and use to line a 20cm pie dish. Spread chocolate hazelnut spread over base of pastry. Drain pears and arrange over pastry base. Roll remaining pastry out and place over pears, pressing edges together. Cut two steam holes. Bake at 190°C for 35 to 40 minutes or until pastry is cooked.

Serves 4 to 6.

Coconut Macaroon Peach Pie

3 egg whites

¾ cup sugar

1 teaspoon almond essence

½ cup coconut

¼ cup readymade caramel sauce

FILLING

1 cup whipped cream

½ cup prepared cold custard

415g can SPC 100% Peach

415g can SPC Peach Slices in Light Syrup

Beat egg whites until stiff. Beat in sugar and continue beating until mixture is thick and glossy. Mix in almond essence and coconut. Baking-paper-line the bottom of a 20cm loose-bottom cake tin. Spread the mixture over the base and sides to form a shell. Bake at 180°C for 30 to 35 minutes or until shell is cooked and lightly golden. Leave to cool. Spoon filling in roughly. Arrange peach slices on top and drizzle with caramel sauce.

FILLING

Mix cream, custard and 100% peach together. Drain peach slices.

Serves 6 to 8.

Maple Nut Pie, Chocolate Cinnamon Pear Pie and Coconut Macaroon Peach Pie

SUMMER BERRY PIE

6 cups mixed fresh or frozen berries such as blueberries, raspberries, blackberries

2 tablespoons cornflour

2 tablespoons water or drained berry juice

1 1/2 cups flour

1/2 cup custard powder

1/4 cup icing sugar

250g packet Kraft Philadelphia Cream Cheese

1/4 cup water

Icing sugar

Thaw berries if frozen. Place berries in a saucepan. Heat gently. Mix cornflour and water together and mix into berries. Cook until mixture boils and thickens. Leave to cool. While filling is cooling, place flour, custard powder and icing sugar in the bowl of a food processor or bowl. Cut in cream cheese until mixture resembles coarse crumbs. Add enough water to form a stiff dough. Roll dough out on a lightly floured board and use to line a 20cm flan tin or dish. Reroll pastry off-cuts and use to make decorative shapes. Bake with pastry shell. Bake pastry shell blind at 190°C for 15 minutes. Remove baking blind material and return pastry shell to oven for 3 minutes to dry out. Cool then fill with berry mixture. Arrange pastry shapes over berries. Dust with icing sugar and serve.

Serves 6.

CAPPUCCINO PIE

BASE

200g packet chocolate wheaten biscuits

50g melted butter

1 tablespoon instant coffee powder

FILLING

1 cup milk

2 tablespoons instant coffee

1/4 cup sugar

1/4 cup cornflour

2 egg yolks

TOPPING

2 egg whites

1/2 cup sugar

1/2 teaspoon cocoa

Chocolate sticks

Crush biscuits until medium-fine crumbs in a food processor or a thick plastic bag. Pour in melted butter, add coffee powder and mix to combine. Press mixture into the base of a 20cm springform pan or loose-bottom cake tin. Refrigerate while preparing filling. Pour filling into base. Spread over topping and bake at 190°C for 10 minutes or until just starting to colour. Dust with cocoa and garnish with chocolate sticks.

FILLING

Whisk milk, coffee, sugar and cornflour together. Heat, stirring constantly, until mixture boils and thickens. Remove from heat and mix in egg yolks. Pour into prepared base.

TOPPING

Beat egg whites until stiff. Gradually beat in sugar until mixture is thick and glossy.

Serves 4 to 6.

Summer Berry Pie and Cappuccino Pie

59

Quick 'n' Easy

OPERA HOUSE TART WITH RUBY SAUCE

PASTRY

1 cup polenta

1/2 cup cornflour

1/2 cup flour

1/2 cup sugar

150g butter

1 egg

1 tablespoon raw sugar

FILLING

2 x 415g cans SPC Pear Halves in Light Syrup

1 1/2 cups red wine

3/4 cup sugar

1 cinnamon stick

5cm piece lemon rind

4 whole cloves

Place polenta, cornflour, flour and sugar in the bowl of a food processor or bowl. Mix to combine. Add butter and mix or rub in until mixture resembles coarse crumbs. Mix in egg to make a stiff dough. Refrigerate while preparing filling. Cut dough in half and press dough into the base of a 20cm round loose-bottom cake tin. Press or lightly roll second half to a 20cm circle. Place cooked drained pears on pastry. Top with pastry circle. Sprinkle over raw sugar. Bake at 200°C for 25 minutes or until pastry is lightly golden and cooked. Serve hot with wine sauce and cream.

FILLING

Drain pears. Mix pear juice, wine, sugar, cinnamon stick, lemon rind and cloves together in a saucepan. Bring to the boil. Add pears and simmer for 5 minutes. Drain pears from wine mixture and set aside to cool. Bring wine mixture back to the boil and heat for 8 minutes or until sauce is reduced by half. Serve warm.

Serves 4 to 6.

PEAR TART TATIN WITH GINGER CREAM

415g can SPC Pear Halves in Natural Juice

50g butter

1 cup sugar

1/2 teaspoon ground ginger

2 sheets flaky puff pastry

1 tablespoon melted butter

Drain pears, reserving juice. Cut pear halves into thin slices. Melt butter and sugar in a large frying pan with a metal handle. Heat until bubbling. Arrange pears, cartwheel fashion, in the butter mixture. Sprinkle over ginger. Brush one pastry sheet with melted butter and place second sheet on top. Cut pastry to fit the diameter of the frying pan. Place pastry on top of pears and cook on top of stove over a medium heat for 15 minutes. Remove pan from stove and place in a 200°C oven for 10 minutes or until pastry is golden. Remove from oven and turn tatin onto a serving plate. Serve hot with Ginger Cream.

GINGER CREAM

300ml cream

2 teaspoons icing sugar

1 teaspoon grated lemon rind

2 tablespoons reserved pear juice

1 teaspoon ground ginger

Whip cream until soft. Mix in icing sugar, lemon rind, pear juice and ginger until combined and the preferred consistency.

Serves 4 to 6.

Opera House Tart with Ruby Sauce and Pear Tart Tatin with Ginger Cream

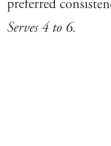

APRICOT TART

Other fruits can be used in combination with or instead of apricots and the sponge flan case can be replaced with a pastry case.

2 teaspoons grated orange rind
¼ cup orange flavoured liqueur or 1 teaspoon orange liqueur concentrate
250g pot Kraft Soft Philadelphia Spreadable Cream Cheese
200g prepared sponge flan
2 x 415g cans SPC Apricots in Natural Juice
1 tablespoon gelatin

Beat the orange rind and liqueur or liqueur concentrate into the cream cheese. Spread into the base of the sponge flan. Drain apricots, reserving 1 cup of juice. Strain juice into a small saucepan. Arrange apricot halves over cream cheese mixture. Sprinkle gelatin over juice. Leave to swell for 5 minutes. Stand over hot water until gelatin dissolves. Cool, then pour over apricots. Leave until set.

Serves 6 to 8.

CITRUS TART

If limes are available use these instead of oranges for this citrus tart.

400g packet sweet short pastry
3 eggs
1 egg yolk
1 cup low-fat cream
2 teaspoons grated lemon rind
1 teaspoon grated orange rind
¼ cup lemon juice
¼ cup orange juice
¼ cup sugar

Roll pastry out on a lightly floured board and use to line a 20 to 23cm flan or pie dish. Bake blind at 200°C for 10 minutes. Remove baking blind material and return pastry shell to oven for 2 minutes to dry out. Beat eggs and egg yolk until light and fluffy. Lightly beat in cream, rinds, juices and sugar until combined. Pour into cooked pastry shell and bake at 150°C for 30 minutes or until filling is set. Serve at room temperature.

Serves 4 to 6.

Apricot Tart and Citrus Tart

Quick 'n' Easy

INDEX